Teach Yourself Mapmaking

for my father

Previous publication:
Circumnavigation (Smith/Doorstop Books 2002)

Acknowledgements
Some poems have been published in *Magma, The North, Other Poetry, Poetry Review, The Reader, The Rialto, Scintilla, Staple*; and also in *The Allotment: New Lyric Voices* ed. Andy Brown (Stride 2006); *Waymark*, The Middlesex University Press Literary Prize 2005; The Ware Poetry Competition Anthology 2005, The Bridport Prize Anthology 2004 and Lancaster Litfest Competition Anthology 2003.

Special thanks are due to Rupert Loydell and Mike Barlow.

Teach Yourself Mapmaking

Jane Routh

Smith/Doorstop Books

Published 2006 by
Smith/Doorstop Books
The Poetry Business
The Studio
Byram Arcade
Westgate
Huddersfield HD1 1ND

ISBN 1-902382-80-3

British Library Cataloguing-in-Publication Data. A catalogue
record for this book is available from the British Library.

Designed and typeset at The Poetry Business
Printed by Charlesworths, Wakefield

Front cover photograph 'The Cartographer Revisits the Day-
Job' (2006) by Jane Routh
Author's photograph by Mike Barlow

Distributed by Central Books Ltd., 99 Wallis Road, London
E9 5LN

The Poetry Business gratefully acknowledges the help of Arts
Council England and Kirklees Culture and Leisure Services.

CONTENTS

A beautiful art,

the triangle, drawn on damp paper
over the imprint of old voyages
spread across the rolling table.
The pencil soft, but finely pointed.
A quiet clack of parallel rules;
the marks on paper light, transient.
Erased by evening.

And always a certain triumph –
the triangle, small: against
the pull of current and the push of wind
in all those elements, those crests,
that dark gust, in all this nothing,
this sea, here, this hull, this moment
we are here, we are lurching on

and we can fix the next wave
or the next, hand-held numbers
spinning round to starboard, hovering
then swinging back to port, the gut
plunging and the eyes almost closed,
assessing a moving needle
against a moving landmass.

A beautiful art, to draw on worn charts
and one you feel not far removed
from Loki reading his ravens' flight
when he discovered Iceland,
nor so different from how six'ern crews
rowed back to land they couldn't see
by set and pitch and scend and smell,

so that when you key in waypoints
for the autopilot, the waves that engulf you
come close to regret, and you wonder
– as is the way when you're at sea –
what if the waypoint for home
were seasickness, were risk, or skill, or age;
what if the waypoint for happiness, pain?

The Red Cow

They were reaching north up the coast
for shelter in the lee of Skye, stiff with cold
after another day of stinging rain
and waves so short and steep they'd had to take
every sounding more than once,
when the last of the squalls raced away east
and a brief evening sun poured colour
back into the sea, so they all saw it: a cow
two cables off on the starboard quarter,
sitting on the waves and chewing a cud of tangle,
the curve of her spine and bony haunches
darker than a Hereford's, a rich red
among the *Glas Eileans* and the *Sgeir Dubhs* –
a single eccentricity in their meticulous work
and one unremarked by the Hydrographer.

The Half

It was a flat sea, an idle sea: none of the tide-rise
and rollers we were used to up north. Blue
I'll grant, but slicked all over with chrome.
It was an empty sea: no boats and no coast
but a thousand foot rock called Redonda out west.
Or east – the sun was unreadable, shadows were wrong:

I felt like a bird on migration must feel
if the map in its head goes blank. The compass
was set on some shimmer of heat that could change,
if you stared, to a black palisade with missing planks.
And it was eight knots easy: the same breeze every day
rose with the sun then dropped as fast as the tropical night.

Too fast to fish, I'd have said.
I couldn't believe the weight of the sinker we needed,
streaming the lure's vermillion stripe and tinny glint
through the wake, away out of sight. The line
was cleated, too heavy to hold – you had to watch
for a change of angle, even a splash somewhere astern,

like whatever it was we saw as the line veered taut
on the quarter, and down. We pulled together
hand over hand over hand, the line tangling on deck,
the line heavy, then stalled, then surging, then light, lost? –
no, still something silver and we hauled over the transom
a half-fish, a ragged black-bloodied butchering of our tea.

The half-fish had a jutting jaw and tapered head;
it could have been four foot, or more; might have been
this one? or this? on our chart of edible and toxin-free.
Iridescent bluish-green was good, but we had no second dorsal,

no warning sign of lateral line curving down the diagram
on its scaly side. In the end we believed what we wanted

and sawed off steaks, threw torn flesh overboard,
saved the head for bait. I dipped a wary bucket
backwards through the metal lid of the sea,
swilled the deck and the gear again and again
until water ran clear through the scuppers and rinsed away
all knowledge of what it harboured underneath.

Sea Change

My best days were flat calm. Clear skies but the air cool
and the swell dropped away with the morning tide.
Say, off the coast of South Uist, a scent of heather from the land.

High, Rockall, drifting slowly north I wrote in the log.
At the bottom of the page, in the box for notes
Razorbills and guillemots whistle and growl like hinges in need of oil.
They dive and they disappear dive and disappear.
No mention of what the heart knows.
No signal here was a day to salt down for the memory.

Now I'd probably want something else. Certainly you did:
your best days were rougher – slamming into seas,
a couple of reefs in the main, and visibility
(spray or heat haze or rain) to test your navigation.
You were bored while I trailed mackerel feathers
or let out the main as if every ounce mattered.

Maybe there were no such things, best days
– you know how it is:
High dissipated; complex Atlantic low moving rapidly east.

Foresight

Seaboots and a shirt are strewn on the rocks.
A dinghy makes quick surges, falls back and surges
at the end of its painter, as if anxious to be off.
A man and woman are eating mackerel
cooked in wet newspapers on the embers
of kindling from the oakwoods –
they burn their fingers on the smoke-sweet flesh
and in their own ways they love each other.

They're young and fit and everything is possible;
tomorrow they plan to walk twenty miles
along the coast. What could I say to them
if I were to send a small whirlwind – the sort
that flares from nowhere on warm summer days –
to stir the last of their fire and leave a sign?
They haven't even glanced upwind
to check the weather for their long sail back.

It's already late afternoon: an evening breeze
could air its forecast among the oak leaves.
The tide's about to turn – wavelets
running up the shingle could hiss presentiments
or, since this is my poem, I could walk
down from the woods, smile and say Nothing
will ever taste as sweet as those mackerel.
Without hindsight, would they believe it?

There's nothing remarkable about the day
to them – no point in warnings: with their
unbroken bodies and unknowing hearts
they would not be able to understand.
All we can do is watch, and know what we know
as they spread and stamp the ashes of their fire,

then slip the painter and wade out
gasping and laughing at cold shocks of sea.

Tomorrow, they say, they'll walk along the coast
as far as Glenelg and back over the mountain.
The sails flap briefly; snap into shape.
They slip quietly up the loch past the island
where seals are hauled-out, dry and pale. A few
turn their sad gaze on the goose-winged boat
then roll back in the last of the sun and wait
to be floated off by the rising tide.

Waiting

Those of us who like to be on time
spend a long time waiting for those
who are not. Those of us who return
from the mountain by the safe route
we took out, spend hours watching
for those on a short cut across the river
or along the coast. We worry about them:
have a warm drink ready and dry clothes.

Sometimes, the sky clearing, the islands
floating back to the horizon, darker now
and nearer, we wonder what it would be
to be other than ourselves.
We know that (one day) there will be a gift:
one day, an otter will slip through the rocks,
shake herself, and run close by
into the bracken at the foot of the cliff.

If we see her, we shan't tell. Sometimes
we wonder whether it would be better
to drift on the wind like the willow-down,
careless. Yet it was we who saw the ravens
fly down to the tideline, prospecting,
we who saw the fan of a black wing stretched
and rayed with emerald and amethyst
when the sun broke through.

Teach Yourself Mapmaking

I shall need a small boat – not too heavy –
with an outboard and lugsail and oars;
two boathooks and a leadline (the coast
is what I'll like most). If it is possible
let her be clinker-built and painted yellow.

I shall need many large sheets of paper.
Pencils. Notebooks. A house on the shore.
I should like it to be traditional, its back
to the wind and a window to watch the tides.
Remember not to show me a map.

If you cannot find me an island
a peninsula will do, but not too large.
Do not mention its shape. If it has hills
that are too high or too rough
I shall leave them blank.

It will be best if you take me there
in the dark. Unload well-being on the beach.
They say illness is a dream of contrary;
remembered, it can do no harm.
Dare it to stalk me there.

I'm thinking of the depth of an inlet,
an outcrop of rock, the track
that stoats and foxes use
 – but none will have names
unless I walk out in the morning

and record my own history over theirs.
Why go so far, if that is all?
The island will define itself.

I will use my own name
once, and write it small.

It will take as long as it takes.
When you come to collect me
you can bring your map and compare
mine. An aerial view will be interesting;
mine is ground level.

Sula Sgeir

The island does not bear her name
though the one her brother lived on
ten miles east bears his.

Legends concern the devils
the sainted brother overcame
to build his church –

windowless, half-underground,
a byre roofed over with turfs.
Yes, he'd soil enough for turf, and oats

but where she lived
Atlantic gales fling waves
clear across the island rock

and all that grows is June's
unexpected froth of sea pink.
The only food is winged.

The brother lorded other creatures,
beached a whale by prayer
so he could ride, not row, the seas.

She's forgotten and unsainted
though she opened up her ribcage
for a shag to nest inside.

Blessed House says the map
of the place they found her,
riddled through by the winds

as the island's riddled through
by the sea, all hollows and caves
and the smell of the solan goose.

The Tombolo

Without that voice in his head, he can hear the wind
and the quiet suck of little waves;
he hears a skua's *uk-uk-uk*.

Morning, he thinks, but he has lost his north.
A dark, dense haar. He can see only four
of his footprints in the sand; sea rocket.

The waters at his feet slowly divide; a thin band
of pale sand stretches away from the shore
into the nowhere of fog.

An act of faith to walk this narrow spit out into the sea?
Oh I think he knows this is no one-off miracle:
sandhoppers jump ahead of his toes;

a man like him can read the angle of wavelets
for split tides; knows the phalanx of bonxies
he hears can't see him.

He'd walked to Rome when he was young, but allow
a few doubts now, eight hundred paces out
and no sight of where this sandbar leads.

He'll breathe more deeply as the sand widens,
loosens, and his feet sink into dunes –
the other side,

where he'll find good green grazing underfoot
when the fog burns off: a high flat island,
drongs and fangs of rock to seaward.

Sheep. A well. An ancient temple
in need of nothing but an altar.
Some saints have all the luck.

St. Etheldreda flees south, to land where there'll be a
yacht club in thirteen centuries' time

There would have been a boatman.
Only a local man would know the tides
– strongest where the water is deep –
and shifting mudbanks behind the island.
The boat would have been small:
we could ask our friend the fisherman.
A beggarwoman and two nuns.

It would have been night, slack water
unless she willed the flood-tide not to ebb
for seven full days and nights like last week
when she cut her husband off.
Spoken instructions were against the rule
but a man able to read wind in the clouds
and the shifts of brown waters
would have noticed the beggar's slim hand
hesitating at her neck. And put it
from his mind: a capsized boat has no rights.
No lights, just his thick hands on the oars
feeling for the pulls of eddy and tide
and pausing for the noises of the night.
The nuns and the beggar would not have heard it
the way he did, the watery swish of reeds
but they would have felt the wind drop,
the boat no longer rocked by waves
as he dipped quietly between the tall grey plumes.
This is The Haven. He would have noticed
the smallness of the beggar's feet on the soft brown mud.

If we were to cross her, she'd cheat
and perform a miracle, press her stave,

say, into the ground, until it thickened   branched   leafed:
Fraxinus excelsior.
She played by the old rules, and never mind
explanations: there were no doubts.
See, here is the foundation stone.

Teach Yourself a Lost Language

Take two drams and a native speaker
at an old oak table that used to be an altar years ago.
Sit back in the fresh gust and blow of it,
ripples catching the sun. Put down your pen –
look how his mouth holds on to the vowels
for the taste of salt fish hung to dry on the line, reluctant
(think of it, he says, with three As) to laaave them be.

Watch his fingers tap percussives
as he tells his generations and counts out
six houses on the street where he was born:
a master mariner, a circumnavigator,
and the man you'd see once every couple of years
back from the whaling to mend the roof
– a small world, South Georgia next door.

Now he is speaking of things for which
there are no words in our language.
Don't ask for translation. He can read you well –
this is a simple word, but full of compassion.
When he sees that you are lost, he'll leap up
and demonstrate how his grandfathers
would open their doors to a stranger,

sweeping you in, sweeping you in
making you welcomed, and at home.

Elsewhere

A man is gazing out to the horizon.
It's low tide, the blue-grey seascape
rippled inshore with evening darkness.
Haze casts doubt on distances.
I should have mentioned that the man
is naked: I was intent on his looking.
He is also standing in seawater
up to his thighs, very still with this
looking, still as a truncated torso
on a plinth. And there is a second man,
tiny, much further out, and another:
they too look towards the horizon,
they too stand quite still, the incoming tide
around their ankles; maybe they have found
a sand bar. In the gloom of last light
they also appear naked, watching
another place infinitely far off.
If my eyes were better, I could tell you
whether that furthest cipher
were merely a perch marking the margin
of a channel, or yet another man –
the sea could be full of watchers:
the body cannot simply return
to its old haunts. I do not want to miss
whatever it is the watchers look for;
I do not want to turn round
but if someone is behind me
he may notice a figure at the edge
of the water. He may notice the figure
is looking; that the figure is not yet wet.

Tell Me What Else

Now tell me why. Tell me about greed.
Show me how to think about infinity.
How far does war go down with you?
Make me a list of what counts. Explain
why you think the moon's the same size
as the sun: your answer's who you are.
Say how three brothers trouble sleep,
turn, and draw their brown cloaks close
as they approach the arch – whether
they visit from another life, or whether
they're already dreamed and something
in your brain has named them wrongly.
No more about roses or snowdrops
but tell me about your sly animal self
among the dry ochre grasses of winter.
Or tell me about the moment when you sit
on a boulder in the river and you are the river,
you are the alders and the early morning air
and the deer who doesn't see you, high-stepping
among cobbles at the crossing place
on such thin legs.

Transit of Venus

Somewhere above the heavy haze, Venus
is transiting the sun. The other side of the world
a man casts off his moorings, searching for warmth.

Here, small birds fall from secret places:
lucky ones find a twig to cling to, forsythia
or rose; fasten on like mutant blooms.

Those that land on the grass whirr
like cockchafers at a light. Little Lucifers,
they can only descend, not rise up:

they have not yet learned fear,
they open their wide mouths, O yes
they'd believe anything I dropped in there.

They have not yet learned the sun can blind,
that to leave the nest is to cross a pale,
that when you ask, it will no longer be given.

Segue

Bats who dropped moth wings and furred parts
on my doorstep in the night are sleeping somewhere secret.
A three-day secret's divulged, the redhead's promise
broken. A branch breaks under its weight
of unthinned apples: grass quails, then accepts the windfall.
A Grassy Knoll breaks into seven conversations,
most of them in Texas – one of those things
the tongue can't leave alone. A tanker in ballast
leaves Hormuz astern, discharging waters
from a world away before it enters harbour.
On a small boat a man leaves harbour queasy
and reefs down, already doubting the course
biro'd on the back of his hand. Don't doubt
that children could come into the story at any time:
it's already story-time five hours east of here,
and five finger execrcises in G minor trip
through an open window hung with wisteria
while thousands more windows are opened to let in
thousands of cats, some of which have been stalking the night,
some of which have been killing moths.
This is no surprise: there is no such thing as coincidence,
only a failure to imagine enough possibilities.
Never mind butterflies, this was not a poem
in which it was good to be a moth, not even the one
whose moon-led radar my kitchen light reduced to spirals
until it smudged the windowpane with rufus wing-dust
you could mistake for a comet trail tonight
were you to focus on the stars.

Night and Day

Strange, to wake back in middle age, stiff and sore.
If we inhabited our lives the other way round
with the colour and contrast turned up full,
Pharoah's armourer offering to cut off our rings
with bolt cutters, against a backdrop of gold pyramids,
no they're palm trees, I mean doors,
everyone we know using everyone else's name
and acting out of character with intimate strangers
kicking up divots from long ago, the ground tilting
the car hurtling backwards down the track
even though it's in first gear, no brakes at all,
we'd be exhausted and long for our dream days:
the kettle in the right place, breakfast always the same,
our weekly shop, even the slow pulse of the seasons
lending a little glow of predictability;
we'd love the washing-up bowl, the settee,
grey days, no wind, and especially fog.
A small price, the body, we'd say, taking our pills.

Heart

Underwater a seal's heart slows down
fifteen-fold, I wrote in my book.
I wanted to know everything
there was to be known about hearts.
On the facing page, I listed
his family's phone numbers.

He wasn't underwater, he was
under sedation and maybe that was
like water to him: I watched his heart
earth-tremor under his skin
and always so long before the next,
no matter how hard I willed it.

•

In the evening when I ring
he's back in High Dependency,
oxygen forced into his lungs.

I press the wrong button,
catch his usual hesitation:
Sorry I'm not able   to take your call

I hang out washing in midsummer dusk,
do not care if it rains in the night.
I wonder how they stop a heart?

•

Breathe, damn you.
Never mind it's hard:
if sucking on a plastic tube
to shift a yellow ball
towards a smiley icon is
what will make you well,

then suck, damn you.
Don't cross your legs.
Don't hunch your shoulders
in an old-man-slouch:
the wind might change.

•

A garden warbler flies at the window, falls
stunned. Since Job's God was not averse to bets,
I gamble your life on its. It gapes, pants for air.
I'm tired; I need something to eat.
When I look again, it's nowhere.
Deus absconditus.

•

My day off. Hours I would have spent
on the motorway, I'm joyriding the tractor.
It's the erratic beat of the human heart,
I wrote in my book, enables it to adapt.

•

I tuck you into the car as if I know what I'm doing.
You are a glass of water I must not spill.
All I remember of the drive home:
flax on the Fylde, blue fields and a blue sky.

You fear sleep, your dreams too vivid.
That's normal, I say, no idea if it is.
The wind drops; a yellow moon lifts off over Bowland.
When I check, you're still breathing.

•

The heart of a blue whale
weighs two tonnes.
All that blood, imagine,
all that heartache.

Short Sentences Without Electricity

A. All I can see of you is fireglint on glasses and belt buckle.

B. Shelved books bite their tongues until my torch-beam bewilders them.

C. Not one candle, they say, to be had in the village.

D. Days last longer without electrical demands.

E. How eager we are for the week to move on, for evenings with moonlight.

F. Carrying frail tea-lights, we are mindful where we place our feet.

G. The stove gobbles logs; we feed it hourly.

H. As well as heat, the stove gives light; the lamp, also.

I. The toast, you said, was ingenious; but crumbs are everywhere.

J. Judged by the sound of a splash, my whisky is larger than usual.

K. The old kettle fits the stove exactly; comes to the boil at its own pace.

L. A poem's just legible held close to a flame.

M. In the dark mushrooms are washed by feel.

N. We offer our neighbour a share: hot food, storm lantern, candles.

O. The room smells of paraffin, old-fashioned.

P. Familiar pinpricks of light have disappeared across the fells, as if no one's there.

Q. Such quiet – no hum from fridge or immersion heater.

R. How we re-value nightsight, and touch.

S. Smuts from the lamp salt my page.

T. Talk fills the dark before bed.

U. The umbrella plant sheds a leaf: the smallest sounds startle.

V. Your voice tells me where you are; we should wear white.

W. Wick up, wick down, the lamp has constant attention.

X. Except for the wind, the only noises are our own.

Y. Yellow pools of candlelight guard entrances like Chinese Door Gods.

Z. One goes gladly to bed.

Eleventh Hour

There are leaves still on the trees
near the mountain hut, Mont Blanc framed
perfect against blue sky. In Yellowstone
you can see only stars. It's night
in Auckland too: those are its lights
glittering across the bay from Devonport.

The South Pole's out of action, all turbulence
and wind. Mawson Station's on:
portacabins in primaries, rock, snowdrifts.
No one outside. Pale sky almost green.
Ascencion looks abandoned: 27° – dawn I think –
a white dory pulled up the hard, a wave.

Macquarie's frozen, a Sisley of lilac
greys and green, but Antarctica's left behind
its sound effects: sea ice breaks and cracks
unstoppably, a Weddell seal yawns.
Nothing from Nuuk; and in the dark, Denali's
lost to Anchorage's light pollution.

Ah yes, Bagdhad. Out-of-date
as you'd expect. A green shop sign,
an ordinary side-street. No one's about.
The text is Spanish – if I have it right, it says
all people are collaterals.
Everyone. Everywhere.

Armistice Day 2003

Issue

It covers the whole table, this chart
of people who need no introduction,
though most I don't know.
Smoothing out its folds brushes off
my unique and solitary self, leaves me
an amalgam of births and deaths and squabbles
across two centuries of marriages
and re-marriages, of cousins marrying
and children by a sister's husband's uncle.
Interlocked lines of Marys and Janes
finger down through the years until here
I am, bottom right. *Born*, it says;
No Issue, it says and leaves a small box
empty for when I die.

I'd not thought of myself
like this, a dead end on a diagram
of false starts: *No Issue, No Issue*
repeating under ten of a row of siblings;
No Issue putting an end to a column claiming
undisputed title to the orchards.
It stops and starts like snakes and ladders.
Except there's no ladder I can climb back up
to snake down differently so we'd need
a longer sheet of paper, or even
so I could be finished off like this man
I'd not heard of until today (back three
across five and two down to bottom left)
followed only by a question mark.

Handed Down

Great Aunt Louie had no children. My mother says
she had spare rooms where you could stay,
always wore black and a chatelaine
with a little leather pouch for all her rings.

Lily had the one with two emeralds and a ruby
set with pearls. Ethel's was opals. My mother got
the turquoises though one of them is green
and should be changed; she passed it on to me.

Because of the way mother complains *and you
never wear it*, I looked out its tiny heart-shaped box
and tried it on. A perfect fit
but on my right hand an improbable thing.

There were oars in my dream, and close-ups
when I looked at my hands and thought
how long and thin my fingers had been
when I was as young as myself in the dream.

Or maybe I was dreaming Aunt Louie's hands,
handed down with the yellow gold in the dirt
trapped round the clasps. I have no children
but I have spare rooms, and I am who I dream.

All My Dead

The lately-dead return in the night, balance
their over-large heads on thin bones and ask
Do you think I am going to die? Yes, I say, Yes.
Their faces are crumpled like a newborn's.
I hear them screaming under the bed.
It is not easy to imagine what it is like
to exist only in someone else's memory.

The long-dead are quieter. They leave their toils
in ones and twos, step up to say their names.
Sometimes they bring a landscape with them.
Souls of their dead infants cling to the womens' skirts
like patchy fog; even they do not remember
their faces. Subsistence is what they care about:
they don't mind what you invent.

And those not-yet-dead who know they
are next in line, the ones with grandchildren,
make ready, and talk among themselves about
how someone should have photographed
the moor before it was fenced, or haytime even:
this is the closest they come to saying
what they mean. Then they start to repeat themselves.

Definitions of Happiness (i)

To the right, the front room
too good for all but the dead
who left their best china
in the glass-fronted cupboard
when they were laid out there.

Wood-grain painted on the door.
I have been in others too:
all horsehair and crochet,
antimacassar and flying ants.
They smell of must. A thick hush.

•

Talk resumes in the middle room.
I don't live here though once
do sums at the table
and get one wrong.
It's always dim: the window
gives on to a passage, washing,
a bicycle leaning up the brick.

•

Beyond the middle room,
the back kitchen, warm,
the ur-room

where coal comes up from the black cellar,
where small bowls of peach slices and evaporated milk
are carried carefully from the white cellar on special Sundays.

Clack of the yard door.
All comers known, to time,
listened for,

everyone coming up the passage
ducking the smalls and the sheets.
Another bicycle leans up the first,
another raincoat's hung behind the door,
cycle clips, a peaked cap and badge,
another chair pulled close to the range,
purple and green spills, the kettle
swung in over the coals, then out,
the brown teapot on the trivet,
sleeves rolled, collar off, stud
into a square Goss dish *A Present from Blackpool*
and pegged all through with *do you remember,*
the rag rug, *that was a good suit, had it when his uncle died,*
hardly worn – the words invented, but generic.

•

Five doors along, an identical room
and a daughter-in-law who makes
everything. Party-dresses. Twigs
set with yellow jasmine flowers
of moulded wax. Silver balls on iced buns.
She has beautiful teeth,
she smiles and smiles pink lipstick,
clicks when she walks.
Click click, the irons on her legs.

•

The crush,
kettle, brown teapot,
the window steamed up:

37

interiors can be relied on,
constant through the tellings; figures
less so, shrinking over time.
What did you see of them anyway,
too familiar to remark?

•

The allotment with rows of loganberries to be lost in
was to me, then, self-evident happiness.
I never asked.

But what's memory
before you knew that was a question
and it could be asked?

The Sisters

Both my father and my mother had a sister
who died of TB. I knew neither: they died
childless and young. Any photos are lost
though it's said if it weren't for my hair
I'd be the image of my father's sister.
All I know of this woman is her name
and the fact that she died during the war
and if she had not died
she would have married my father's best friend
except that he, too, died in the war.
My mother's sister died in a hut in the garden.
I used to imagine a ramshackle shed
under the old and sprawling trees which fruited
huge ungainly apples as sour as Bramleys.
There was a row of pinks along the path,
old-fashioned, with split calyxes and fringed petals,
and a strong sweet smell of cloves.
I've seen them in garden centres
but struggle to grow mine from slips
off a cutting I had from my mother.
I only persevere because of that garden,
its hut, and the war, though these are not
my memories but ones I've inherited,
and nothing connects those two women
who never knew of each other
except the way a niece they never imagined
threads their lives together, briefly,
as she washes garden soil from her hands.

The Spires

It no longer reaches the three words forward
to the end of a sentence, but my mother's memory
stretches as far back as whooping cough,
the racking sound and the exact words
her mother spoke: Be silent, child –
others need their sleep for work.
Two rooms, ten children, all gone but her.
She likes to recite the names and savour
their deaths in their gardens: a family blessing,
to die forking the earth. She remembers
the day her mother died,
remembers saying Dr Creasey you must
save my mother. She was lifted out
through the window on a plank and no last words.

That was in a strange country where men
were called Hereward and there were no hills.
Conversation was ruled by The Forty Foot.
To shorten a car journey into the fens,
I was told to count spires. There was a place
where you could see thirteen.
Sometimes my mother can name them all,
her parents buried below one, the eldest sister
by another – that grave's been kept decent,
my mother says, sodium chlorate, so it'll last.
When I ask about her mother's grave
she's unsure, says you'd need good weather.
Yet again I stop short, cough
instead of asking where she will go.

Made to Measure

Will Taylor buried one of my grandfathers
for twenty-nine pounds eighteen shillings and tenpence;
if you were a village joiner, you did the undertaking too.
My father was a joiner, but that was in a town,
so when he was out drinking with Will
and word came there'd been a death
and Will asked him to give a hand to measure up,
it may have been the first time my father

had seen a corpse, which may explain why he can
still demonstrate exactly how Will Taylor
pulled a piece of string from his waistcoat pocket,
stood the younger man at the feet with one end,
stretched the string along the body, then knotted it.
Took the width and tied another knot,
bent down to sight the belly and tied a third.
This had been a big man.

I can see the two of them in that upstairs room
with the curtains closed, their boots loud on the boards.
Their walk down the fen has not quite cleared the ale
and tobacco from their heads. A paraffin lamp
by the bed throws Will Taylor's shadow across the wall
as he pulls the string back and forth between his hands,
shakes his head and announces soberly
he doesn't have a board that long.

The edge of disapproval in my father's voice
is for the string, the lack of rule; he gives away
nothing of how he felt when Will Taylor reached down
a pile of books from the wardrobe top,
told him to pull back the corpse's toes, and handed him
the books to wedge between the soles and iron bedstead
so the corpse would set an inch or two short, just right
for two elm boards at the back of his joiner's shop.

Another Country Churchyard

Indian summer, humid and hot;
I've brought all the wrong clothes.
Heat haze. Just you, me, this churchyard wall
and a few fields. Yours is a strange country
with its flat plains, wide rivers.
Deep valleys are what I know.

It would be strange these days to you too:
The Dog and Duck re-named;
your four- and six-acre fields on the warp
ploughed into a single sweep of dusty stubble;
mud-caked willows on the new embankment
dwarfed by Drax and all its vapours.

Maybe the slow-closing squeal of the iron gate's
not changed. Three men came back
but not your James. They called it celebration,
those thousands of changes, a full peal
of Oxfords, Kent Treble Bob and Plain Bob
with ex-sapper Jennings on the Tune.

You would have heard *that*, Joseph:
three hours they rang for the dead,
grim-faced and blinded by sweat –
even, let's suppose, by tears. Those bells
marking your eternity, the way hands
on the church clock once counted your toil.

I'm a stranger, Joseph, to this country of yours
with its heavy end-of-season greens,
kicking my heels on the wall and willing
that gilded face to strike familiar. *In such an hour
as ye think not* is all you have to say, while I
buff up the bright whorled conkers from all around you.

To Mow a Meadow

When I first learned fractions at school
it was with men mowing meadows:
if eight men take two days, how long for one?
I was town child, imagined a man
with a lawnmower and his dog.

Now it's a fine thing to mow a meadow
especially in an evening breeze before the dew –
fast downhill towards the wood, uphill to clear sky
or out along the shoulder with the view upstream
where the fells fold in above the river.

Someone else would take less time. I've always
small triangles to finish off, never the precise rows
of a Nash painting or my neighbours' fields.
I'll turn off the tractor when I've done, stand
to watch the fields fall vast and still.

The cut I like best is a single swathe
curving down from the garden gate
through the hay to a stile by the Old Wood.
A narrow path changes the way you see
the land, draws your eye deeper in.

Years back, Skirrow's nephew set a scythe
for my height and reach. The sweep
that was easeful in his hands was struggle in mine:
I hooked and flattened the grass, rarely felt
the silvery grassfall of a perfect stroke.

If it takes one great great granddaughter
two hours to mow a meadow, how long
for eight great great grandfathers, cursing
flies and blisters yet cursing more those machines
like hers that turned them out of their lives.

In Praise of Land Drains

On a fine day after rain, the wind dropped, listen
anywhere moles have burrowed echo chambers
and you'll hear splashing underground.
It's days like today, driven rain
straight off the Irish Sea and coat seams letting water,
you look for the spurting geysers of a blockage

and dig on the down side. Keep digging,
three foot, maybe four, and cut a step.
Watch your wellies. Get in the hole
with that fast and muddy water
and channel it downhill. *Pass the crow bar.*
Hear it ring on stone. *Now we're getting there.*

Someone – Robin, say, for whom it's named –
dragged this meadow out of moorland.
Hacked down gorse, scythed rushes, turned it
with a hand-held plough. Picked stones and piled them.
Dug deep: under sod, under subsoil,
down into the solid clay. And drained it.

Tunnels of boulders, roofed over with slabs,
overturned turfs and backfill. Built to last
a lifetime and every lifetime evermore.
He couldn't have imagined the weight
of machines, end-of-season contractors
driving over land too wet for hay.

As good as moats and castles on a beach.
This time there's a fine spraying fountain
when we hit the spot. *Shift that slab!*
and the whole seething, swirling mass
gurgles off down Robin's drain, still sucking
the land back into shape just as he knew it would.

Keeping an Eye

Dusk. The young geese shut up for the night,
boots on the doorstep and the keys hung up.
A light at the top of the wood across the valley:
no track there. The beam wavers between trunks.

Watching the neighbours I said, when the man
selling binoculars asked. I should have said
For birds or *For when I'm at sea.*
He looked at me and kept a note of my address.

Dusk, and a couple of stars: what they call
nautical twilight. A red glow in the stove,
a whisky. I took my eye off that light and lost it.
Then find them: a muck-spreader and two tractors.

The spreader must have got stuck where
land drains are broken at the edge of the wood.
Keys. Boots. Winch and chains from the barn.
No one round here's surprised when you turn up.

On Guard

As if it's just another meditation on the day
I sit out the long twilights with a gun.

No hardship: pheasants clatter into roosts,
blackbirds alarm among the bushes, an erractic bat or two,

sheep, owls at each end of the Old Wood,
a car changing gear a mile down the valley:

the noises of the night arrange themselves in order
then silence settles with the dew across damp grass.

Night falls with a little wiffle of wind from the wrong direction.
Some things don't sleep. Rustle: it could be

breathing somewhere behind. Don't turn.
Watch the gap in the gorse for a grey shape to shift

until all that's visible is my imagining.
Leaving, I lumber in a landscape where people don't belong.

A touch at the neck. How silly, that willow hangs low.
Speak softly to where my flock of shadows will be.

The barn gate: enough light now from the house
to follow the fence. How ordinary it is, the kitchen, the warmth.

Night after night, and nothing. The weather
turns. No creature will be about on a night like this.

So sure, but by morning a white irruption ripples over the orchard.
So much down: the guard gander.

The geese stand on one leg under the damson trees,
heads under wings, at rest in the sun. Just another afternoon.

Routines

Now and again at this time of year I hear
wild geese fly west, their calls torn from the sky
with leaves from the trees, though never before at dusk
walking my own flock back from the river and wood
and never so low as these – one long line so low
I can count them *twenty*, hear their everyday gabble *thirty*;
their lines break, vee and veer west *seventy*, lift
– at that height they will see estuary and moss –
are gone. I stop, wait for my flock to fly off
but these birds who'll stand one eye tilted to a jet
at 30,000 feet neither look, nor pause in their routine:
only I, filing through the orchard, ache for an uprush of air
and twilight's steady sheen at the horizon and I –
I fold my wings and fasten the gate, follow the flock
along the track, as I do, every evening at dusk.

Her First Flight in a Microlight

See how wrong the maps are now:
the river's slow curve has changed direction
and what's happened to the road beyond the scrub?
That sudden brilliance must be a pond:

those ripples are a coot's, folding down
the bur-reed where she'll cup her eggs
– there's nothing retting in the shallows,
no riven oak strips, hazel wands.

Farm Farm Farm insists the map
along a band of nettles by the moor,
Sheepfold Sheepfold but no one's about,
no excited dogs behind a flock.

Quarry Quarry Shafts Quarry
it says across those rushes and the gorse.
No carts or voices, no bow-saws
or charcoal burning in the woods –

the only smoke is from that barn. Look:
a magpie's at the roof-light's fleeting sun-glint.
It taps, then hammers, hammers,
hammers down for sorrow on the glass.

Like Speech

He must have been dead long since
but they still blame Skirrow if a chicken
disappears, unless it was clearly a fox.
Even so there are those who say he kills
like a fox, strews feathers to fool you.

I saw him once – I think it was him –
sack over his shoulders to keep off the rain,
binder twine holding his trousers up.
Dark, I'd say, but it could have been shadow:
he was off through the trees as I turned.

No one's exactly sure about his looks.
He never spoke. Some will tell you he was dumb,
but when you hear two owls calling at dusk
they'll warn it's Skirrow after rabbits.
Birdsong round here often sounds like speech.

You can smell charcoal-burning when it's still
but no one coppices Robin's Close Wood.
The laughter's nothing but yaffles and jays;
coughs and squeals could be foxes or deer
though I heard a weeping I couldn't pin down.

After I asked around who'd set a scarecrow
where I'd ploughed, that field fell still and bare.
Once a gate I'm sure I'd fastened swung open
when my aching arms were full of kindling:
it doesn't do to think about these things.

His brother was a merchant; the farm was let
though Skirrow never left: this was all he knew.
They say he lived above the shippon:

eight goose wings and five goose feet were found there
that John Wilson claimed his own; he knew the marks.

There was a ladder with some missing rungs
behind the hay: I climbed up one time and found
a lumpy armchair and a cup that had
its motto chipped away. Two words were clear:
leaves and *was*. It struck me that the floor was clean.

View Over Burnmoor

He's walking where a cobalt wash shadows
burnt sienna on the moor, a small figure
five hundred yards away, not everyone
would notice. You'll see him more clearly
at the end of the day when low sun
works up the fields' flat slabs of ochre
into vivid planes. I've watched him for years
there, under that hill shaped like a hoof.
You won't see him at night, not even
when I leave curtains open for a Hare Moon.
In the dark he no longer haunts
the brushstroked distances; he must
double-back along the lampblack gulley,
vault the top bar of that gate, then drop
– quick and quiet as a spider on the lino –
into my kitchen. I keep a mug of tea poured
ready on the table. That's the Old Road
you're on, I'll say, tell me how long it took
from here to there; put me in the picture.

Last Days

A south wind always put out the night's fire.
He slipped barefoot through the hedge for dry leaves.
He was about before anyone else:
there'd be horse mushrooms in Parrocks Field.
It was a fine day, mild and bronzey,
a good season for rabbits. He'd snares to check.

Yesterday he'd caught a hare by the leg – electric silk
with the energy of a thousand devils – and let her go.
She'd taken no harm. (You'd have freed her too
if you'd once watched hounds chase her in a mad, wide circle
until she crouched in sudden stone-stillness
so the dogs on a moving scent ran clear over her.)

I like to think this is how Skirrow's last days
would have been. This, or something like it – unplanned
until a whim or blackbirds' alarm calls in Collinsons Wood
urged him out, and landscape and weather shaped his day
– though who knows how he would have voiced it
to himself, a man who had not spoken since childhood.

There are those who say it's only stories –
how could anyone survive like that, and all those years?
No records name him, though the parish always gave
its paupers a decent burial: Skirrow must have died
like the birds, invisibly, under a hedgerow. Where he lived
was marked in census ledgers *uninhabited*.

Landscape with Figures

I don't think of him now if I walk by the bridge:
that land's changed hands, run to a tangle
of bramble and thorn; elms long dead,
barked, bleached and fallen, but that's OK:
the two of us long gone our separate ways.

·

There was a place above the river I'd go
when I was sad. You'd sit against an oak
legs dangling from a cliff where the river
undercut the bank. The drop wasn't so steep
you'd get vertigo, but deep – a hundred feet or so.

I've cried there, but it's hard to concentrate
when the river and the trees take no notice
and things rustle. I read somewhere we weep,
on average, seventeen litres in a lifetime.
I like that idea: a way to measure unhappiness

– my half-bucketful of sorrows disappeared
in a landslip with the oak, and nowhere left
to stand and say *This was where.*
And that's all right too, as if the landscape
timed it to accompany my life.

·

You'd think all the land round here
would have moments of my life tucked in like this:
where a fox got Jones; where we picnicked
those midsummers before any of us died,
but there's so much no one can recall:

the air, the shades of evening, the person
you were who noticed these things. It's as if
today's demands have overgrown them,
events that don't concern us now gone
as irreversibly as the wood's fallen leaves
have turned to leafmould. In the end,
it's only landscape.
            The Old Wood, oblivious,
slowly recovers itself with a few early-purples
then a helleborine – and another –
just off the path near the wicket above the river.

Wavelengths

These ash have done well. I describe them
ghost-grey in the winter light.
The man from the radio asks
what I did before planting trees.
This is the track of an old road, I say,
that once zigzagged through the wood
to a ford – listen, the river's high
after all that rain. The man from the radio
wants to know why I plant all these trees.
I make my footsteps crack broken twigs
and say, so many white willows blew down
in last night's storm I'll try alder instead,
and pause near the landslip for mauve bloom
on the buds of a sapling that deer
can't get to because of the briers. He asks
how I feel when trees fall, or deer eat them.
Look – There's one! a white rump bouncing
another! between trunks at the edge of the wood.
I am not sure what he sees where I point
– you catch rhythm not shape –
so I show him this is an elm bole long dead
that's sprouted new wood, this
is dead-hedge round coppiced hazel,
here are its catkins still closed tight
because this month's moon is the Ice Moon,
but he wants to know what makes me
do this. I tell him it's as natural as breathing
to pull a whip through this T-cut I've made
in damp earth. This is the sound of roots
being spread and turf folded back and tamped down.
He asks if I'm obsessed. No. No, it's what I do.
When he asks whether I am Christian,
whether 'owning' trees is about power,

nothing else comes into my head to say.
The man from the radio
                        slips, but I catch him:
he's come to no harm; it's only mud.

Mid-November Proofs

Sacks of grain in the barn, logs split and stacked,
redwings and fieldfares raiding the hollies and thorn.
Most of the leaves have coloured and gone.
Everything's ready, and still the winter rains and cold
don't come. Only the birches hold fast to bronze halos
waiting their chance to be remarkable.

Every time my oldest friend comes here he says
he can smell this house. Stone? Woodsmoke?
He shrugs: Itself; how it always is.
The poet whose proofs I am checking knows
nothing of this. Six hours west and in his bed,
he's unaware of the sheets quietly lifted

and piled page by page into a still life
where low slants of yellow sun lick over
the cut-apples-and-pips patterned lamp
on great-grandfather's table, a postcard from Bora Bora,
an old marriage certificate with a woman's name
crossed out and her sister's written in.

Maybe the poet whose proofs I am reading would like
the way leaves blow in whenever I open the kitchen door.
As I do. Don't ask: everyone knows
when you visit a hermit on the mountain,
he's always just gone, *Gathering berries,*
his apprentice might say, waving vaguely at the mist.

Definitions of Happiness (ii)

Sheet-tin walls, but the corner posts
deep set in concrete, and a fine stone chimney
running up the gable. (No, no: tin's not cold
lath-lined and stuffed with sheeps' wool.)
A doorway, a window and a view.

As hidden from landward by the cliffs
as invisible from seaward for the reefs
– but a good clear back-bearing
for an incoming boat (the east end
of the island just open on the outer rock).

A wall round a small patch of flat land;
holly and a rowan keeping witches at bay;
roses, apple blossom, a barrier of wolfbane
across the door – rampant blue. A species
of happiness, this solitude,

the spring chattering through the rocks?
Ask the archetype, the rusted iron bedstead;
ask the cuckoo – only he returns year after year
drawn, the way dreamers are drawn
by unbelonging and by chance.

The Reedbed

What was I hoping for, what was I trying to find
that September afternoon, skimming across
the Humber under slender cables to the other side.
The past of course, something to say this is how it was,
even something forgotten of my own, a view perhaps,
to account for how I imagine ships trawl
the top of an embankment beyond a kitchen window.
But there were no ships. All that brown water
and just a green-hulled light-float with its silent bell.

What was there to see in a village of closed doors
gone about its twenty-first century commute.
The church was locked. Not one headstone shared my name.
Behold, he taketh away; who can say unto him, what dost thou.
A gable end stopped me – not familiar, but seen before.
I'd gone because I still love the colour of bottled plums,
the press of golden flesh through crimson juice against glass.
I did find the orchards, now The Orchards, meaning
executive houses instead of trees. And one old brick wall.

On the sign outside The Ferryboat, one man rows another
across the estuary, all that distance in a little yellow hull.
But where the boatyard was, ploughed stubble.
The creek silted, narrowed and shallow.
No voices, no hammering, no trace of planking or a nail;
nothing to write home about as my father would have said.
Only the reeds, their grey plumes and dry leaves
lilting in the sun with a sound like running water
tell how it was then. The tall, plumed reeds.

The 'Elizabeth Ann'

i.m. John Routh

Now all the other visitors have left
I can hear the ache of parched timbers.

Look: here I am on CCTV
running my hand along the strakes
and tapping on the copper nails
you hammered in.
New warps are neatly coiled along her decks.

Listen: the alarm; uniformed footsteps
running up the stairs. Too late:
my foot's on the gunwale,
I'm on board,
pull the tiller over hard.

She casts herself off.
                                    The Haven unsilts.

I gybe and ease the sheets
and sails that have hung slack
in the airless hall for years
gulp salt air   and belly out
in the following wind.

She storms through the Hessle Whelps
for the open sea. There are no charts
for sands that shifted then
but who cares, who cares,
it's in the blood. Isn't it?

Lagan

*Lagan: materials thrown overboard but attached to a buoy
or marker for retrieval at a later date.* (Merchant Shipping Act 1995)

1

Food and clean water, the day's rituals with geese.
Collar up, hail in fists and drifts.
Snowdrops on the bank under the oak,
                                        not wild –
doubles, somebody's pride
                        and joy.
Mine too, green rosettes crammed under long petals
shedding a century or more of rain.

2

A century of rain at Lily's funeral.
Have you come after school? she asked, the day before she died.
That's right, I said, old enough for children of my own at school.
That's right, which it was in its own way,
                                        time gathering together its things.

On her sideboard under a print of Hylas and the Nymphs,
the mahogany tea box that's in my kitchen.
I should like to say I think of her
                                every time I fill it.
But I don't.

I see her now and again,
                        tiny in a hospital bed.
Thousands of words. And I remember five.

3

Not one word of my grandfather's.
His bread board, fire irons, two willow pattern plates
so much in use here I can't imagine them there.
But say *Binbrook* and he's settling a trilby against the breeze,
Northcoates, Caister, his overcoat flapping, *Holme-upon-Spalding Moor.*
All those east coast aerodrome names on a Landranger map.
Binbrook, men's talk.

Tithe map of 1848:
a garden in the corner of a field
                      where my vegetables are.
I fork up broken stems of clay pipe and earthenware rims,
my leeks north-south
               like James Taylor's, Skirrow's and Ann Twisaday's.
Daffodils showing, not theirs – older, the small ones *flore pleno.*

Worked traces all over this land:
drains and pathways, blackthorn at the top of the wood,
holly on the cop, hazel and elm coppice
                      for hurdle, bobbin and board.
You were buried in elm: it endures underwater.
Shipwrights used it for keels.

5

The round table my father lifted out of the boot was oak.
He was particular I remember his grandfather made it.

I sanded it by hand,
               rubbed in six coats of oil with wire wool,

his boatyard apprentice.

Six coats. See, John,
it's in the family.

6

Generations, before my ash trees are fit to fell.
Few straight enough for furniture,
                                    winds snapping stems,
shoots spurting sideways.

Brackenwood Nurseries, whips, customer to collect.
That was 1994.
Since then I've grown my own,
                                    ash seeding itself
3 million to the acre.

7

February fill-dyke, power cut and south-westerly gale.
The great ash on the eastern skyline felled in the night.
Nobody's tree,
                    a wildling at the boundary by the stile.
Everyone's waymark.